THE PLANETARY SOCIETY

T0024021

CASTING SHADOWS

SOLAR AND LUNAR ECLIPSES WITH
THE PLANETARY SOCIETY®

A NOTE FROM BILL NYE

The excitement, beauty, and wonder of outer space is up there for everyone to enjoy, including you! When the Moon lines up with the Sun and with us here on Earth, amazing things happen—eclipses. They're beautiful and a little bit weird. Open this book and see for yourself!

The Planetary Society® empowers people around the world to advance space science and exploration. On behalf of The Planetary Society®, including our tens of thousands of members, here's to wishing you the joy of discovery.

Onward,
Bill Nye
CEO, The Planetary Society®

TABLE OF CONTENTS

EARTH, THE MOON, AND SHADOWS

Have you ever seen the Sun look black? Has the Moon looked red? These are some of the amazing things that happen during eclipses.

A total solar eclipse (*left*) and a total lunar eclipse (*right*)

What are They?

When you stand in the sunlight, you have a shadow. Sunlight cannot go through your body. That's why you have a shadow!

Earth and the Moon have shadows like people do.

Earth and the Moon also have shadows. They have big shadows because they are huge! An eclipse is when one of them enters the shadow of the other.

A lunar eclipse happens when the Moon enters Earth's shadow. The word *lunar* means "something having to do with the Moon."

A solar eclipse happens when Earth enters the Moon's shadow. The word *solar* means "something having to do with the Sun."

Lunar and solar eclipses usually happen a few times each year. Each time, they can only be seen from part of Earth.

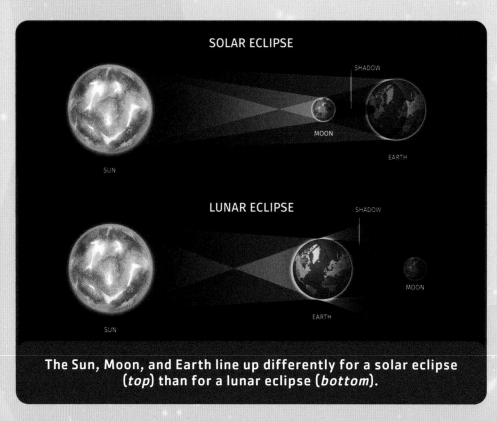

SOLAR ECLIPSE

SHADOW

MOON

EARTH

SUN

LUNAR ECLIPSE

SHADOW

MOON

EARTH

SUN

The Sun, Moon, and Earth line up differently for a solar eclipse (*top*) than for a lunar eclipse (*bottom*).

Earth, the Moon, and the Sun must be in a line for an eclipse to take place. The word *syzygy* refers to three bodies in space that are in a straight line.

A Past Look

Until a few hundred years ago, many people thought eclipses meant something bad was going to happen. People did not know why they happened. And they did not know when they would happen. A suddenly dark sky could be very scary!

Now we know eclipses are because of shadows. Scientists predict exactly when they will occur.

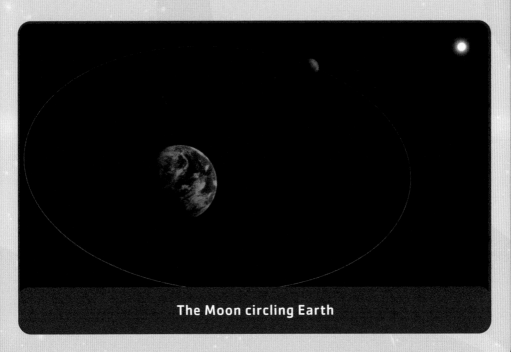

The Moon circling Earth

How Earth and the Moon Move

The Moon goes around Earth. It takes about thirty days or a month to circle Earth. Earth and the Moon together go around the Sun. It takes one year for them to circle the Sun.

Eclipses only occur when the Sun, Earth, and the Moon are in a line. But Earth and the Moon are always moving. They only line up a few times a year. So eclipses don't happen often and don't last long.

The Moon circles Earth, and both the Moon and Earth circle the Sun.

A BIG FIND ● ● ● ● ● ● ● ● ● ● ●

People used to think the Sun moved around Earth. But in the early 1500s, scientist Nicolaus Copernicus (*below*) found out that Earth moves around the Sun. His finding was later proved by other scientists.

CHAPTER 2

LUNAR ECLIPSES

Light from the Sun is called sunlight. The Sun makes sunlight. Light from the Moon is called moonlight. Moonlight is sunlight that has bounced off the Moon.

A full Moon

From Earth, we can see dark or bright areas of the Moon. The area of the Moon that is in daytime looks bright. The area of the Moon that is in nighttime looks dark.

Part of the Moon in daytime

Part of the Moon in nighttime

As the Moon goes around Earth every month, we see different amounts of bright and dark areas. These changes are called the phases of the Moon.

PHASES OF THE MOON

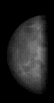

NEW MOON	WAXING CRESCENT	FIRST QUARTER	WAXING GIBBOUS

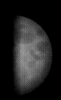

FULL MOON	WANING GIBBOUS	THIRD QUARTER	WANING CRESCENT

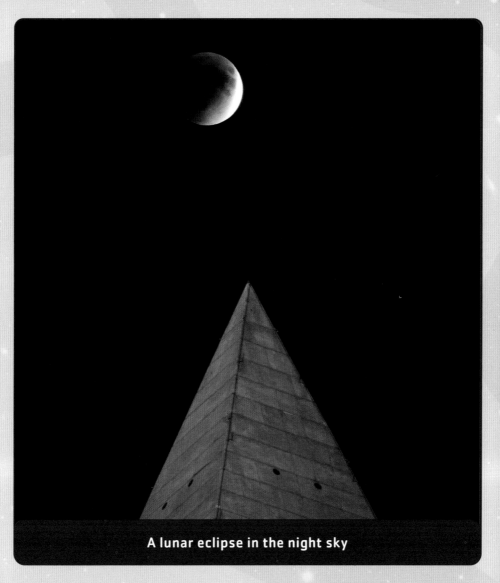

A lunar eclipse in the night sky

A shadow can also make the Moon dark. A lunar eclipse takes place when Earth comes between the Sun and the Moon. This blocks sunlight from reaching the Moon. Earth's shadow can cause the daytime parts of the Moon to darken.

Types

Sometimes the Moon goes through only the top or bottom of Earth's shadow. Part of the Moon gets dark. The rest stays lit by sunlight. That is a partial lunar eclipse. Other times, the whole Moon will go into Earth's shadow. That is a total lunar eclipse. It lasts about one to four hours.

A partial lunar eclipse

A total lunar eclipse

When it begins, only part of the Moon is dark. The Moon keeps moving until all of it is in Earth's shadow. The whole Moon is dark at that time. Then the Moon starts to move out of the shadow. More and more of the Moon is lit up by sunlight.

The Moon darkens and can look red during a total lunar eclipse. This is because some sunlight bends through Earth's atmosphere. The atmosphere is all the gas that surrounds Earth. Red light is the best color at getting through the atmosphere.

The Moon may look red during a total lunar eclipse.

PROOF EARTH IS ROUND ● ● ● ● ●

During a lunar eclipse, you can see that the shape of Earth's shadow is round. The ancient Greeks used this as evidence that Earth is round.

How to See One

People can only see lunar eclipses when it is nighttime. When the eclipse happens on one side of Earth, people on the other side will not be able to see it. This is because it is daytime for those people!

People watching a lunar eclipse

People can take photos of a lunar eclipse.

Lunar eclipses are safe to look at with just your eyes. You also can watch one by using binoculars or a telescope. An adult can help you look for when the next one will take place.

The number of lunar eclipses you can see from where you live varies from year to year. In most years, you will be able to see at least part of one if the sky is not cloudy.

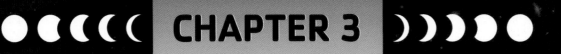

CHAPTER 3

SOLAR ECLIPSES

A solar eclipse happens when Earth passes through the Moon's shadow. The Moon comes between Earth and the Sun. It blocks out the Sun.

A partial solar eclipse

Types

There are three types of solar eclipses. The Moon never completely blocks the Sun in a partial solar eclipse. In an annular solar eclipse, the Moon does not cover the entire Sun but leaves a ring of the Sun around the Moon.

An annular solar eclipse

The Moon completely blocks the Sun in a total solar eclipse. When it begins, the Moon moves in front of the Sun. It keeps moving until the Moon totally covers the Sun. This is called totality.

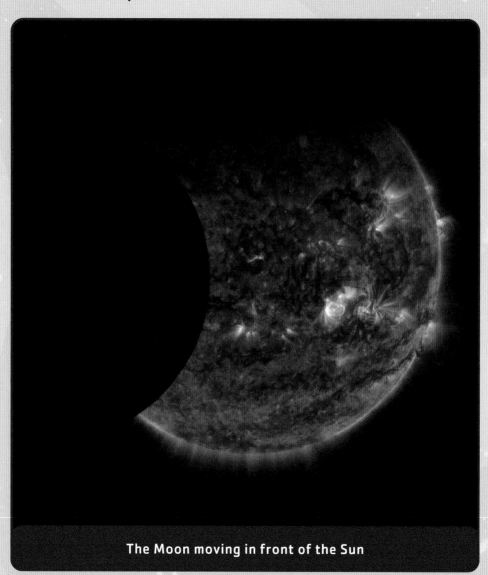

The Moon moving in front of the Sun

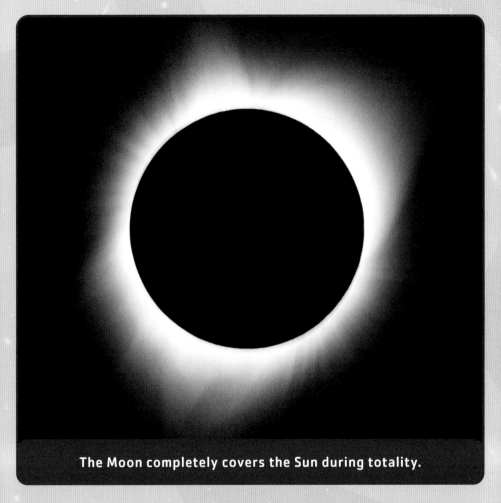

The Moon completely covers the Sun during totality.

Some weird things happen only during totality. The sky becomes dark like night, except at the horizon. Birds may stop singing. The air gets colder. And the outer part of the Sun's atmosphere can be seen. It is called the corona and looks like fuzzy lines.

Totality lasts less than seven and a half minutes. After totality, the Moon moves out from in front of the Sun.

How to See One

The Moon's shadow only covers a small part of Earth. So only people in certain places on Earth can see a solar eclipse. This is different from lunar eclipses that can be seen from a very large area.

Most people will have to travel to see a total solar eclipse. Partial solar eclipses cover a larger area but still do not happen often.

As the Moon moves and Earth spins, the Moon's shadow moves across Earth. A total eclipse can only be seen from a path that the center of the shadow follows. Outside that path, people will see either a partial eclipse or no eclipse.

People watching a solar eclipse

The safest way to view a solar eclipse is to put a pin hole in a sheet of cardboard. Then stand with your back to the Sun. Hold the cardboard in the sunlight. It will project an image of the Sun onto the ground. Or you could hold a sheet of paper behind the cardboard hole to view the image.

People can project an image of the Sun onto the ground to safely watch a solar eclipse.

There are also special eclipse glasses you should wear to watch a solar eclipse. They are not regular sunglasses. Regular sunglasses are *not* safe when watching a solar eclipse.

An adult can help you look for when the next solar eclipse will happen. You may have a chance to see a few from where you live.

SAFE FOR DIRECT SOLAR VIEWING

People wear special glasses to watch a solar eclipse.

MARS HAS ECLIPSES

Rovers on Mars have taken pictures of solar eclipses. They happen when one of the planet's two small moons pass in front of the Sun.

A mars rover (*bottom*) and photos of a solar eclipse on Mars (*top*)

Future Eclipses

The Moon is slowly moving farther from Earth. It moves at about the same rate your fingernails grow!

In the far future, the Moon will be too far away to cover up the Sun completely. That means there will be no more total solar eclipses. But that won't happen for about a billion years from now! You will have more chances to see one.

The Moon will one day be too far away to completely cover the Sun.

Keep an eye out for future eclipses!

Lunar eclipses and solar eclipses are very different. But both kinds are amazing to watch. If you see one, imagine how the Moon is moving through space. Be safe and have fun!

GLOSSARY

atmosphere: the gases surrounding a planet, moon, or other body

day: the time it takes a planet to spin around once

gas: a state of matter with no fixed shape or volume

lunar eclipse: an event where Earth comes between the Moon and the Sun, causing the Moon to enter Earth's shadow

moon: an object that orbits a planetary body

planet: a big, round, ball-shaped object that only goes around the Sun. Our solar system has eight planets.

solar eclipse: an event where the Moon comes between the Sun and Earth, causing Earth to enter the Moon's shadow

totality: the period when the Moon completely covers the Sun during a total solar eclipse

year: the time it takes a planet to go all the way around the Sun

LEARN MORE

Betts, Bruce, PhD. *Super Cool Space Facts: A Fun, Fact-Filled Space Book for Kids*. Emeryville, CA: Rockridge, 2019.

Find Solar & Lunar Eclipses in Your City
https://www.timeanddate.com/eclipse/

Hirsch, Rebecca E. *Mysteries of the Moon*. Minneapolis: Lerner Publications, 2021.

Kingston, Seth. *Eclipses*. New York: PowerKids, 2021.

NASA Space Place
https://spaceplace.nasa.gov

The Planetary Society: What Is a Solar Eclipse?
https://www.planetary.org/articles/solar-eclipse-guide

INDEX

PHOTO ACKNOWLEDGMENTS

Image credits: NASA/Carla Thomas, p. 4 (left); NASA/ARC/Brian Day, p. 4 (right); Martin Barraud/OJO Images/Getty Images, p. 5; Macrovector/Shutterstock, p. 6; Garor/ Shutterstock, p. 7; grayjay/Shutterstock, p. 8; traveler1116/E+/Getty Images, p. 9; Ann Stryzhekin/Shutterstock, p. 10; Vxfour11/Wikimedia Commons (CC BY-SA 4.0), p. 11; Peter Hermes Furian/Shutterstock, p. 12; NASA/Aubrey Gemignani, pp. 13, 23, 24, 29; Stephen Rahn/Wikimedia Commons (CC0 1.0), p. 14; NASA/Joel Kowsky, p. 15; Giuseppe Donatiello/Wikimedia Commons (CC0 1.0), p. 16; Jake Herman/Shutterstock, p. 17; Carl De Souza/AFP/Getty Images, p. 18; VCG/Visual China Group/Getty Images, p. 19; NASA/Bill Ingalls, p. 20; Kevin Baird/Wikimedia Commons (CC BY-SA 3.0), p. 21; NASA/ SDO, p. 22; Michael Wheatley/Alamy, p. 25 (left); Sean Bromilow/Alamy, p. 25 (right); Brian Farrell/Moment/Getty Images, p. 26; NASA/JPL-Caltech, p. 27 (rover); NASA/ JPL-Caltech/Malin Space Science Systems/Texas A&M Univ, p. 27 (moons); NG Images/ Alamy, p. 28.
Front cover: Benny Marty/Shutterstock. Back cover: ESO/INAF-VST/OmegaCAM. Acknowledgement: OmegaCen/Astro-WISE/Kapteyn Institute; NASA/Joel Kowsky (lunar eclipse); A013231/Wikimedia Commons (CC BY-SA 3.0) (solar eclipse).

For my sons, Daniel and Kevin, and for all the members of The Planetary Society®.

Lerner Publications Company
An imprint of Lerner Publishing Group, Inc.
241 First Avenue North
Minneapolis, MN 55401 USA

For reading levels and more information, look up this title at www.lernerbooks.com.

Main body text set in Aptifer Sans LT Pro.
Typeface provided by Linotype AG.

Editor: Brianna Kaiser **Designer:** Kim Morales **Photo Editor:** Annie Zheng

Library of Congress Cataloging-in-Publication Data

Names: Betts, Bruce (PhD), author. | Planetary Society.
Title: Casting shadows : solar and lunar eclipses with The Planetary Society / Bruce Betts.
Description: Minneapolis, MN : Lerner Publications, [2024] | Includes bibliographical references and index. | Audience: Ages 7–10 | Audience: Grades 2–3 | Summary: "The year 2024 is set to have multiple solar and lunar eclipses. But what do you know about eclipses? With engaging diagrams and photos, readers will learn all about eclipses in an approachable way"— Provided by publisher.
Identifiers: LCCN 2023005986 (print) | LCCN 2023005987 (ebook) | ISBN 9798765608975 (library binding) | ISBN 9798765616383 (epub)
Subjects: LCSH: Eclipses—Juvenile literature. | BISAC: JUVENILE NONFICTION / Science & Nature / Astronomy
Classification: LCC QB175 .B48 2024 (print) | LCC QB175 (ebook) | DDC 523.9/9—dc23/eng20230715

LC record available at https://lccn.loc.gov/2023005986
LC ebook record available at https://lccn.loc.gov/2023005987

ISBN 979-8-7656-2456-2 (pbk.)

Manufactured in the United States of America
1-1009645-51575-6/12/2023